INTIMACY
PURSUING INTIMACY
WITH GOD

FOUNDATIONS FOR
CHRISTIAN LIVING
SERIES

BRINGING TRUTH TO LIFE
NavPress Publishing Group
P.O. Box 35001, Colorado Springs, Colorado 80935

The Navigators is an international Christian organization. Our mission is to reach, disciple, and equip people to know Christ and to make Him known through successive generations. We envision multitudes of diverse people in the United States and every other nation who have a passionate love for Christ, live a lifestyle of sharing Christ's love, and multiply spiritual laborers among those without Christ.

NavPress is the publishing ministry of The Navigators. NavPress publications help believers learn biblical truth and apply what they learn to their lives and ministries. Our mission is to stimulate spiritual formation among our readers.

Cover Photo by Cover Images, © 1997 Photo Disc, Inc.

The FOUNDATIONS FOR CHRISTIAN LIVING (FCL) series grew out of The Navigators' worldwide Scriptural Roots of the Ministry (SRM) process. The eight guides in this series reflect the major themes that emerged from ten years of Scriptural study, international dialogue, and prayer. It is the desire of the SRM team that those who follow Jesus Christ be grounded in these fundamental elements of the faith. For more information regarding the SRM process, please write to NavPress at the above address. The FCL series was researched and developed by Don Bartel, John Purvis, and Chuck Steen. The series text was written by Joanne Heim.

Unless otherwise identified, all Scripture quotations in this publication are taken from the *HOLY BIBLE: NEW INTERNATIONAL VERSION* ® (NIV®). Copyright © 1973, 1978, 1984 by International Bible Society, used by permission of Zondervan Publishing House, all rights reserved. The other version used is *The Message* (MSG) by Eugene H. Peterson, copyright © 1993, 1994, 1995, 1996, used by permission of NavPress Publishing Group.

Printed in the United States of America

1 2 3 4 5 6 7 8 9 10 11 12 13 14 15 / 02 01 00 99 98 97

CONTENTS

HOW TO USE THIS GUIDE

*"What comes into our minds when we think about God is
the most important thing about us."*

—A. W. Tozer

Knowing God is of utmost importance. This knowledge is, in fact, a
matter of life and death. When we talk about knowing God, we're not
just talking about head knowledge—doctrine and theology. Knowing
God involves our hearts.

A relationship with God can mirror human relationships. It can be
a distant relationship, a strained relationship, an intimate relationship.
The goal of this book is to help you develop a deep, lasting, and intimate relationship with the God of the universe who invites you to
know Him this way.

Attaining this goal begins with God revealing Himself to us, and
then revealing more and more of Himself as we respond. Responding
to God involves accepting His invitation to intimacy and overcoming
barriers to intimacy. What is intimacy? What encourages and hinders
it? These are some of the questions we will address in this guide.

The FOUNDATIONS Process

The FOUNDATIONS series will help you not merely learn about God but
also grow in your love for Him. Through the FOUNDATIONS process
you'll grow in discovering God, experiencing one another, and serving
in the world. Your group will . . .

> ▶ pursue the mystery of God together and discover ways to draw
> closer to Him
> ▶ grow as you learn to be honest and vulnerable with one another,
> deeply accepting one another

5

▶ become courageous in helping one another at the point of personal need

▶ discover how to live genuinely in this fast-paced, complex world

▶ design ways to serve God together, as a group

The nine sessions in this study follow a three-stage process:

1. Session 1 introduces you to the FOUNDATIONS series. You'll explore three essential elements of the spiritual life on which the series focuses. You'll also begin to develop relationships with the other people in your small group. Session 1 is the same in all FOUNDATIONS studies. If you have recently used another FOUNDATIONS study with your current group, you may simply review session 1 of this study.

2. Sessions 2 through 7 lead you through a variety of issues related to knowing and loving God.

3. Sessions 8 and 9 enable you to take stock of what you've studied and consider what you want to do about it. In session 8 you'll discern how the material applies to you as an individual. Your group will offer feedback and support in following through. In session 9 you'll discuss how the material applies to you as a group. Most of the Bible was written to groups of people rather than to individuals, so session 9 may bring your study alive in ways you did not expect. Session 9 will also help you assess your group's progress in becoming a community as you look at unity, intimacy, interdependence, and mission.

A Modular Approach

Each session is divided into four modules or sections.

OVERVIEW

The overview section briefly describes where the session is headed and what your goals will be. The key issue is stated in the paragraph labeled "So, what's the big deal?" This issue will normally be a point of tension between what the Bible teaches and what we commonly experience. The session will then help your group wrestle through that tension together.

Stating the key issue up front risks preempting the Holy Spirit from guiding your group in the direction He wants to take it, but if you remain open to His leading throughout your individual preparation and group meeting, we believe He'll use the material to minister to you in ways you wouldn't have imagined.

ON YOUR OWN   (30-60 minutes)

This section includes the passages you should be sure to examine before your group meets. You'll find some questions easy; others will stretch you mentally. We've found that a spiritual person is defined more by the internal questions he or she is asking than by the conclusions he or she has already reached. Mind-stretching questions are ideal for group discussion—be prepared for a lively debate! (And don't overlook the *For Further Study* questions, where we've hidden some of the best material in each session!)

As you work through this material, it will be helpful to remember a few "principles of understanding" that relate to learning about God:

▶ Understanding comes through mental exertion (Proverbs 2:3-5). Make sure you schedule enough preparation time to delve into the topic.

▶ Understanding comes through the soul and spirit (John 4:24). Seek God in your spirit as you study, as well as when you discuss.

▶ Understanding comes through the insight of others (Romans 1:12; Acts 17:11). Ask God to make you discerning so you will hear what He is saying to you through each other.

GROUP DISCOVERY   (40-90 minutes)

This will be the discussion portion of your group meeting. It will usually include three sub-sections:
Let's Warm Up: Each group session opens with a question or two to

help you learn about each other. The warm-up questions also help you move from what you were thinking about (or worried about) when you arrived at the meeting to what the biblical texts deal with. These questions put you in touch with the topic in an experiential way, so your discussion is not just sharing ideas but sharing life. The questions in this section always focus on life experiences and are usually fun to answer.

Let's Talk: In this section you'll examine one or two key Bible passages on the topic and discuss what light these passages shed on the central tension of the study. You'll also discuss any questions raised by your individual study. Feel free to bring to the group anything that perplexed or excited you in your individual study.

Let's Act: The questions in this section connect what you've studied to how you live. They often ask you to consider applying what you've learned to your group as a whole, rather than just to your individual life. Application is the reason for Bible study; be sure you allow plenty of time for it.

GROUP WORSHIP   (15-30 minutes)

In order to stress the importance of the worship portion of your meeting, we have set it apart as a special section. Worship and prayer as a group are essential components of the FOUNDATIONS process. Praying and worshiping together can be one of the most faith-building and relationship-building activities you do together. Since many people have never prayed aloud with others before, the suggestions for worship begin gently. Later in the study you'll have an opportunity to plan your own worship times. You may decide to assign one person in the group to plan and lead worship, or you may rotate the responsibility.

In session 4 you'll begin to set aside at least 15 minutes of your worship time to discuss prayerfully and humbly a question often over-looked in Bible studies: "What is the Holy Spirit saying to us?" (This is referred to as *Let's Listen to God*.) You may find it challenging to get past what you imagine God ought to be saying to the group. The experience of trying to discern God's voice will invariably draw your group to a deeper level of intimacy.

Facilitator's Job Description

Leadership is essential to an effective group. FOUNDATIONS studies will go much better if someone in your group takes responsibility to:

1. Launch the group
   ► Recruit people for the group, explaining its purpose and process.
   ► Schedule meetings (with group consensus).

2. Pray regularly
   ► For the individual members in their daily lives.
   ► For the group's growth into community.
   ► For the courage and faith of the group to take the steps it needs to grow in Christ.

3. Build community
   ► Stay in touch with the members, encouraging them to also stay in touch with each other.
   ► Make sure that each member grows in his or her ownership of this group. (This can be done by assigning responsibility—those with responsibility usually experience ownership and genuine membership in a group.)
   ► Help the group move beyond studying to doing.
   ► Maintain momentum and remotivate group members if enthusiasm diminishes.

4. Facilitate rather than lead
   ► Search for vision and direction together, rather than announcing vision and answers. Help the group arrive at its vision and answers. Help people go where the Spirit is leading them, rather than where you think they should go. Remind them that understanding is only the beginning; implementing is the goal.
   ► Teach by asking questions, rather than making authoritative statements. Questions can often accomplish what statements cannot. Questions were Jesus' preferred style.
   ► Draw out the quiet or introverted persons.
   ► Encourage everyone's participation; affirm the different contributions of all.

5. Be content with less than ideal progress
   ▶ Put up with some ambiguity. People never grow in a constant or straight line. Two steps forward and one step back is the norm. Remember what Christ has tolerated in you. Be happy with progress in the general direction of FOUNDATIONS goals.

6. Watch the clock
   ▶ When the allotted time for a given section is over, go on to the next section even if the group has not exhausted its discussion. (It is likely you will need to do this—many of the **Let's Talk** sections have more than enough material to fill the recommended time slot.) Unless you have unlimited time, the group will appreciate being kept on schedule. Don't allow discussion to consume all of your time so that application and worship must be omitted. On the other hand, if you sense the Spirit of God is actively at work, follow the Spirit's leading, not the clock. Look for an appropriate time at which to say, "I sense that God is doing something important here. Is it okay with all of you if we extend our time in this section of the meeting?"

7. Delegate
   ▶ After the first two or three sessions, ask someone else in the group to lead the worship time. Someone in your group is probably gifted in the area of worship and interested in helping the group focus on God through worship. Also, ask someone to lead the Group Discovery discussion. Direct that person to read item 4 in this job description. You could rotate this job around the group. Finally, appoint someone else to be timekeeper. By delegating these three functions, you will encourage all participants to feel like owners of the group rather than spectators.

8. Establish ground rules
   ▶ It is important that everyone in the group has a chance to buy into the rules by which the group will run. Ground rules clarify what the group expects from each person. The most important ground rules are stated on pages 17-18. Be sure to discuss them in your first meeting.

1.
THREE BIG IDEAS

OVERVIEW

In this introductory session you'll examine the three essential elements of the spiritual life on which the FOUNDATIONS series focuses: worship, community, and service. Your goals will be:

▶ To understand and own these three elements—worship, community, and service
▶ To get to know each other by telling a little of your stories and why you've joined this group

Session 1 is the same in all FOUNDATIONS studies. If you have recently used another FOUNDATIONS study with your current group, you may choose to do session 1 or merely to review it and then skip to session 2.

ON YOUR OWN   (30-60 minutes)

Most of us would like to love and be loved better than we already do and are. The FOUNDATIONS series revolves around three fundamental commands Jesus gave to His followers:

▶ Love God with all your heart, soul, mind, and strength (see Mark 12:30).
▶ Love one another as Jesus loves you (see John 13:34).
▶ Love your neighbor as yourself (see Mark 12:31).

In these verses, Jesus states the "big picture" of what the spiritual life is about. We love Him through worship, we love one another through

11

community, and we love others through service. We can depict this threefold lifestyle with the following set of concentric circles:

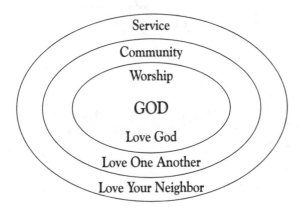

These three commands may be summarized in a single goal for the series:

> *To help you become a community—a small, closely knit group motivated and empowered to worship and serve God together.*

Worship, community, and service form the structural backbone of the FOUNDATIONS process. They will direct your love toward God, toward the others in your group, and toward your neighbors (others not yet a part of your group). At the end of this study, you'll have a chance to summarize what you've learned about worship, community, and service, and to assess your progress as a group toward these three outcomes.

WORSHIP

God's commands about love show that He is vitally interested in relationships and that our relationship with Him should be our highest priority. Worship is the all-consuming, ongoing activity of heaven. We have the inexpressible privilege of joining in the cosmic worship of the King already taking place in the heavenly realm.

When we see God as He is and worship Him, the other areas of our lives begin to work themselves out. Drawing near to God's heart in spirit and truth will inevitably affect our relationships with others.

Hence, worship will become the centerpiece of your group experience. This concentration on God will set your little community apart from a mere discussion group or gathering of friends. While early sessions of this study will include suggestions for worship, feel free to use your entire group's creativity and experience under the leadership of the Holy Spirit as you come into God's presence session by session.

The essence of worship is turning our attention toward God, reflecting His glorious attributes back to Him, and agreeing with who He is and what He has done. God delights to reveal Himself more fully to us as we worship, to satisfy our hearts' desire for relationship with Him, and to give us help for our desperate needs.

God invites us to come to Him with our burdens, needs, joys, and heartaches. In reality, we cannot come to God without our burdens; they are part of who we are. Instead of denying the things on our hearts, we'll find it far more helpful to acknowledge them as fully as possible, commit them to God, then seek Him in His greatness for who He is.

1. When you think of worship, what ideas or images come to mind?
   ☐ lively music
   ☐ majestic hymns or choral works
   ☐ silence and solitude
   ☐ lengthy sermons
   ☐ performers and spectators
   ☐ communing with nature in the woods or by a stream
   ☐ all of life
   ☐ other:

2. On a scale of 1 to 10, how would you rate your most recent experience of worship in terms of how well it focused your heart on God's greatness? Why?

1	2	3	4	5	6	7	8	9	10
dry				okay					awesome

3. Does the idea of worship being the centerpiece of your group experience attract or trouble you? Why?

COMMUNITY

From a centered place of loving God, you'll move outward to loving the others in your group. This shared life is what the New Testament writers mean by *koinonia*: "fellowship," "communion," "partnership," "participation," "community."

> We saw it, we heard it, and now we're telling you so you can experience it along with us, this experience of communion with the Father and his Son, Jesus Christ. Our motive for writing is simply this: We want you to enjoy this, too. Your joy will double our joy! (1 John 1:3-4, MSG)

In the FOUNDATIONS series we assume that dynamic Christian community as described in the New Testament is not only possible but normative for us. When we fail to experience such relationships, we miss the fullness of life that God intends for us. While there are many spiritually important things one can and should do alone, an effective community contributes equally crucial ingredients of life. People in community can:

- ▶ encourage one another in good times and bad
- ▶ ask thoughtful questions when a member has a decision to make
- ▶ listen to God together
- ▶ learn how to pray together and for one another
- ▶ benefit from one another's insights into Scripture
- ▶ acquire a habit of reading the Bible
- ▶ practice loving their neighbors
- ▶ worship God together
- ▶ learn to communicate effectively and solve problems together
- ▶ learn to receive care from others
- ▶ experience the pleasure of helping another person grow

Community in these studies refers to a small group of 3 to 13 people who relate in a certain way. Community in this sense is very different from any organizational form or structure. Matthew 18:20 says, "For where there are two or three who have been joined together into my Name with the result that I am the common object of their faith, there I am in their midst."[1] The individuals together are seeking intimacy with God and fellowship with each other. *Koinonia* includes partnership, participation, and contribution. It implies communication and vulnerability. It is much more than just getting together and discussing some nonvolatile topic.

Jesus wanted His disciples to experience a unique relationship when they came together—unique in their love for and their unity with one another. When genuine love is present, a group has taken the first and biggest step toward real community. This process is not easy. Your group will probably have to resolve a number of relational issues on the road to biblical community.

4. What appeals to you about this description of community?

5. What questions or concerns do you have about this kind of community? Explain.

SERVICE

Any community focused on God loves to serve both believers and unbelievers, just as God does. How could it be otherwise? You'll find that as your group grows in worshiping God and loving one another, the members will intuitively know they need to be helping others. This will be natural.

What may not be natural is serving together as a team and serving the lost—both of which Jesus did and which His followers throughout history have done.

Most of us slowly abandon former friends and acquaintances when we join the kingdom of God. We're not comfortable anymore around those who do not share our new values. Our old friends no longer feel comfortable around us. Somehow we lose the ability Jesus had to be "a friend of tax collectors and 'sinners'" (Matthew 11:19). It is far easier for us to serve those within the kingdom of God than those more distant.

And if somehow we do seek to draw the lost toward Christ, we usually do so as individuals, rather than in partnership with other believers. Consequently, those who need the Savior never experience the powerful influence of a loving community.

The FOUNDATIONS studies will guide your group into these two dimensions: serving the lost and serving together. Serving does not exclusively mean explaining the gospel verbally. Loving our neighbor often translates into specific acts of compassionate service at home, neighborhood, or work. We often serve individually, but this FOUNDATIONS guide will focus your efforts on serving God's interests together. You will not be told what to do; you will not be pushed beyond your point of willing consent. Rather, you will decide together how to put what you are studying into practice outside your group.

6. What thoughts and feelings does this description of service raise for you?
   ☐ Excitement—I'm ready to go!
   ☐ Discomfort—The last thing I need is more on my "to-do" list.
   ☐ Anxiety—I did door-to-door witnessing several years ago and hated it. Will we have to do that again?
   ☐ Ambivalence—I have a strong desire to serve more, but I know it's not easy for me.
   ☐ Confusion—Isn't it good enough for us just to take care of each other for awhile?
   ☐ Relief—I'm glad this isn't just another navel-gazing group.
   ☐ Other (explain):

7. Is this statement true of you: "It is far easier for us to serve those within the kingdom of God than those more distant." If so, why do you think that is?

8. We have stated three priorities: loving God, loving others in the group, and loving others outside the group. What about loving yourself? Do you think this should be a priority ahead of any or all of these three? Explain your view.

 GROUP DISCOVERY (40-90 minutes)

Let's Warm Up (10 minutes)

Beginning with the leader, let each person take one minute to answer question 9.

9. Recall an important friendship from your childhood. Who was that friend, and what was special about that friendship? What bond kept you and that friend together?

Let's Talk (30 minutes)

10. Share your responses to questions 1-8 in the "On Your Own" section. Discuss any questions you have about the three big ideas stated there.

11. Discuss the following ground rules for your group. Feel free to change anything. The objective is for everyone to be content with the result, not for everyone to go along while harboring private reservations.

☐ Purpose: The reason our group exists is to become a community—a small, closely knit group motivated and empowered to worship and serve God.

☐ Participation: I am committed to participating in this community, to worshiping, and to serving others outside the group.

☐ Attendance: I will be here as often as possible. This group will be a priority.

☐ Ownership: I agree to share responsibility for our group goals.

☐ Confidentiality: I agree to keep here whatever is shared here.

☐ Accountability: I agree to give permission to the other group members to hold me accountable for goals I set for myself.

☐ Accessibility: I give group members permission to call me when they are in need—even in the middle of the night. My phone number is. . . .

 GROUP WORSHIP (15-30 minutes)

12. Pray that God would begin to reveal Himself in more of His majesty, power, and direction.

13. Read aloud together this portion of Psalm 89 (from *The Message*):

Your love, GOD, is my song, and I'll sing it!
    I'm forever telling everyone how faithful you are.
I'll never quit telling the story of your love—
    how you built the cosmos
    and guaranteed everything in it.
Your love has always been our lives' foundation,
    your fidelity has been the roof over our world.
You once said, "I joined forces with my chosen leader,
    I pledged my word to my servant, David, saying,
'Everyone descending from you is guaranteed life;
    I'll make your rule as solid and lasting as rock.'"

GOD! Let the cosmos praise your wonderful ways,
    the choir of holy angels sing anthems to your faithful ways!
Search high and low, scan skies and land,
    you'll find nothing and no one quite like GOD.
The holy angels are in awe before him;
    he looms immense and august over everyone around him.
GOD of the Angel Armies, who is like you,
    powerful and faithful from every angle?
You put the arrogant ocean in its place
    and calm its waves when they turn unruly.

You gave that old hag Egypt the back of your hand,
    you brushed off your enemies with a flick of your wrist.
You own the cosmos—you made everything in it,
    everything from atom to archangel.
You positioned the North and South Poles;
    the mountains Tabor and Hermon sing duets to you.
With your well-muscled arm and your grip of steel—
    nobody trifles with you!
The Right and Justice are the roots of your rule;
    Love and Truth are its fruits.
Blessed are the people who know the passwords of praise,
    who shout on parade in the bright presence of GOD.
Delighted, they dance all day long; they know
    who you are, what you do—they can't keep it quiet!
Your vibrant beauty has gotten inside us—
    you've been so good to us! We're walking on air!
All we are and have we owe to GOD,
    Holy God of Israel, our King! (Psalm 89:1-18, MSG)

14. Allow a moment of silence for everyone to focus on God. In worship, you have no agenda but to focus on Him.

15. Beginning with the leader, let each person thank God for one thing he or she learned in this session, or praise God for one aspect of Himself highlighted in your discussion. If you are comfortable doing so, allow for additional, spontaneous expressions of thanks and praise.

Optional

If you think your group might appreciate singing together, ask someone to lead with guitar or other instrument. If no one in your group has that skill, consider singing with a CD; some are now designed especially for small group worship. Be sure the person who leads worship understands that singing is only one aspect of worship, and that he or she should limit singing to the time allotted in your schedule.

---

1. Wuest, Kenneth S. *The New Testament: An Expanded Translation.* Grand Rapids, Mich.: Eerdmans, 1961.

2
IT ALL STARTS WITH A NAME

O LORD, our Lord, how majestic is your name in all the earth!

—*Psalm 8:1*

OVERVIEW

Humans greatly value names. In the ancient Near East, a name was supposed to reflect the character of the person who bore it. To change a name was to change the person's identity. Today our names identify who we are and represent our personality, power, and character. Most people respond immediately in some way when they hear their names spoken with affection, command, or anger.

Virtually every personal relationship begins with exchanging names. To give someone your name suggests that you are open to becoming friends and building a relationship. Among some tribal peoples, one's name is a jealously guarded secret known only to intimate friends and confidants. To reveal your name is to reveal something of yourself.

In this session we will look at some of the names attributed to God in the Bible. By examining God's names and their meanings, we will gain a deeper understanding into God's nature. Your goal is to respond to God's invitation to call Him by name.

So, what's the big deal?
The sovereign God of the universe invites us to call Him by name. What do God's names say about who He is?

1. How do you usually refer to God?

Throughout the Bible, God reveals His names to certain individuals. His names identify Him as God and focus on His attributes—usually in response to a specific need.

The following passages list some primary names for God, highlighting His characteristics. As you read the names and their meanings, circle any phrases or words that jump out to you.

> And God said, "I will be with you. And this will be the sign to you that it is I who have sent you: When you have brought the people out of Egypt, you will worship God on this mountain."
>
> Moses said to God, "Suppose I go to the Israelites and say to them, 'The God of your fathers has sent me to you,' and they ask me, 'What is his name?' Then what shall I tell them?"
>
> God said to Moses, "I AM WHO I AM (*Yahweh*). This is what you are to say to the Israelites: 'I AM has sent me to you.'"
>
> God also said to Moses, "Say to the Israelites, 'The LORD, the God of your fathers—the God of Abraham, the God of Isaac and the God of Jacob—has sent me to you.' This is my name forever, the name by which I am to be remembered from generation to generation." (Exodus 3:12-15)

Yahweh, the root word behind "I AM WHO I AM", is a name for God found throughout the Old Testament. It is His proper name and in many English versions of the Bible is rendered as "Jehovah" or "the LORD." Yahweh is derived from the Hebrew verb *hajah*, which means "to be." As *Yahweh*, God is the One who exists, and who is eternal, absolute, and unchanging. Yet *hajah* is a more active word than our English verb "to be"—it suggests "to be actively present." *Yahweh* is the active, present Creator and the One who gives life.

2. Why is it important that God "will be with you"?

3. How does knowing He is present affect how you live?

> In the beginning, God (*Elohim*) created the heavens and the earth. Now the earth was formless and empty, darkness was over the surface of the deep, and the Spirit of God was hovering over the waters. (Genesis 1:1-2)

El or Elohim (the plural of *El*) is the most common Hebrew term for "god" or "God." Yahweh-Elohim demonstrates His strength, power, and glory in creating the earth.

> "Blessed be Abram by God Most High (*El Elyon*),
>   Creator of heaven and earth.
> And blessed be God Most High,
>   who delivered your enemies into your hand." (Genesis 14:19)

> For the king trusts in the LORD;
>   Through the unfailing love of the Most High (*El Elyon*)
>   he will not be shaken. (Psalm 21:7)

El Elyon means "the Most High God." Derived from the preposition *al*, meaning "above, over, beyond," El-Elyon is above all gods, rulers, and angels. God is the sovereign ruler of the universe.

4. How does knowing that God is the sovereign ruler of the universe, far above your boss, elected officials, or world rulers, affect how you address God when you pray?

When Abram was ninety-nine years old, the LORD appeared to him and said, "I am God Almighty (*El Shaddai*); walk before me and be blameless." (Genesis 17:1)

El Shaddai is God Almighty. *Shaddai* comes from the adjective *sh'day* meaning "enough, sufficient." God is all-sufficient. *Shaddai* is also related to *shadu*, which means "mountains." Promises were often given from the mountains, and God's promises are enough for us.

5. The term "blameless" refers to faithful adherence to a covenant relationship (as opposed to a total lack of sinfulness). What do you think is the connection between God being *Shaddai* the all-sufficient One, and His command to walk before Him and be blameless?

God revealed another name to Abraham when he commanded Abraham to offer his only son as a human sacrifice. Abraham took his son to the place God had commanded, but just as Abraham was lifting the knife, God stopped him and provided a substitute sacrifice:

Abraham looked up and there in a thicket he saw a ram caught by its horns. He went over and took the ram and sacrificed it as a burnt offering instead of his son. So Abraham called that place the LORD Will Provide. (Genesis 22:13-14)

"The LORD Will Provide" is *Yahweh Jireh*, meaning the One who provides for our needs.

6. What are some of the needs in your life that you are trying to fill with something other than God?

7. How is God sufficient to fulfill those needs?

> So Gideon built an altar to the LORD there and called it The LORD is Peace (*Yahweh Shalom*). (Judges 6:24)

Yahweh Shalom is the God of peace and health. The noun *shalom* means "completeness, soundness, safety, welfare, peace, quiet." *Yahweh Shalom* provides us with safety, quiet, and wholeness.

8. The world we live in is far from peaceful. We're surrounded by noise and violence; inside we may sense brokenness or anxiety. What difference would it make to your life if you were connected to a constant source of safety and serenity in God?

> And he [David] became more and more powerful, because the LORD God Almighty (*Yahweh Sebaot*) was with him. (2 Samuel 5:10)

> "Holy, holy, holy is the LORD Almighty (*Yahweh Sebaot*); the whole earth is full of his glory." (Isaiah 6:3)

Yahweh-Sebaot is the Lord of the armies of heaven, the God of war against evil. *Sebaot* comes from the verb *tsavah*, meaning "wage war, fight."

9. Are there any situations you face where you need God to fight against evil?

Then the LORD said to Moses, "Say to the Israelites, 'You must observe my Sabbaths. This will be a sign between me and you for the generations to come, so you may know that I am the LORD (*Qadosh Ysrael*), who makes you holy.'" (Exodus 31:12-13)

Qadosh Ysrael is the Holy One of Israel. *Qadosh* means "holiness, sacredness, apartness" *Qadosh Ysrael* sanctifies us and sets us apart as His holy people. God is holy and separated completely from evil.

10. In what ways do you try to make yourself holy?

11. What would it involve for you to let go and allow God to make you holy?

For the LORD your God is God (*Adonai*) of gods and Lord of lords, the great God, mighty and awesome, who shows no partiality and accepts no bribes. He defends the cause of the fatherless and the widow, and loves the alien, giving him food and clothing. (Deuteronomy 10:17-18)

Adonai means "lord" or "superior." *Adonai* is our master, husband, king, and captain. As Lord, God deserves our submission and respect.

12. Does knowing that God meets all these needs make it easier to give Him the respect He deserves? What makes you say that?

"She will give birth to a son, and you are to give him the name Jesus (*Yeshua*), because he will save his people from their sins." (Matthew 1:21)

Isous (Greek for Jesus) is derived from *yeshua*, which means "salvation, deliverance, welfare, prosperity." Jesus is our salvation and deliverance from sin. Only in Him can we experience true prosperity.

"Therefore let all Israel be assured of this: God has made this Jesus, whom you crucified, both Lord and Christ (*Christos*)." (Acts 2:36)

Christos is derived from the Greek verb *chrio*, "to anoint with oil." It is the Greek equivalent of *mashiach*, from which we get our English word Messiah. The Jews poured oil on the head of a new king at his inauguration. Hence, *Christos* is the Anointed One, the King.

13. Jesus is God and is also revealed through His names. What do these names tell you about Jesus?

For Further Study
What do the following passages teach us about names?

▶ Genesis 3:20   ▶ Ruth 1:20-21
▶ Genesis 17:1-8,15-17   ▶ 1 Samuel 1:20
▶ Genesis 25:25-26   ▶ 1 Samuel 4:19-22

GROUP DISCOVERY (50-90 minutes)

Let's Warm Up (10 minutes)

14. Do you know what your name means? Did it have any special significance to your parents when they named you?

Let's Talk (30-50 minutes)

15. Discuss the "On Your Own" questions. What did you learn about God from His names? About how God meets specific needs?

After leaving Egypt and while Moses was on the mountain receiving the Ten Commandments, the Israelites got bored. They decided Moses was lost and asked Aaron to make a new god to lead them into Canaan.

When Moses came down the mountain and found the people running wild, he broke the stone tablets and commanded the Levites to kill the revelers. God told Moses to go on to Canaan with His angel; God was withdrawing His own presence from Israel because the people couldn't live up to the standard of holiness they would need in order to be intimate with the Holy One Himself. But Moses refused to accept that God's angel was an adequate substitute for God Himself.

16. Read the following passage as a group, underlining words or phrases that describe God's character or actions on people's behalf.

> Moses said to the LORD, "You have been telling me, 'Lead these people,' but you have not let me know whom you will send with me. You have said, 'I know you by name and you have found favor with me.' If you are pleased with me, teach me your ways so I may know you and continue to find favor with you. Remember that this nation is your people."

28

The LORD replied, "My Presence will go with you, and I will give you rest."

Then Moses said to him, "If your Presence does not go with us, do not send us up from here. How will anyone know that you are pleased with me and with your people unless you go with us? What else will distinguish me and your people from all the other people on the face of the earth?"

And the LORD said to Moses, "I will do the very thing you have asked, because I am pleased with you and I know you by name."

Then Moses said, "Now show me your glory."

And the LORD said, "I will cause all my goodness to pass in front of you, and I will proclaim my name, the LORD, in your presence. I will have mercy on whom I will have mercy, and I will have compassion on whom I will have compassion. But," he said, "you cannot see my face, for no one may see me and live."

Then the LORD said, "There is a place near me where you may stand on a rock. When my glory passes by, I will put you in a cleft in the rock and cover you with my hand until I have passed by. Then I will remove my hand and you will see my back; but my face must not be seen."

The LORD said to Moses, "Chisel out two stone tablets like the first ones, and I will write on them the words that were on the first tablets, which you broke. Be ready in the morning, and then come up on Mount Sinai. Present yourself to me there on top of the mountain. No one is to come with you or be seen anywhere on the mountain; not even the flocks and herds may graze in front of the mountain."

So Moses chiseled out two stone tablets like the first ones and went up Mount Sinai early in the morning, as the LORD had commanded him; and he carried the two stone tablets in his hands. Then the LORD came down in the cloud and stood there with him and proclaimed his name, the LORD. And he passed in front of Moses, proclaiming, "The LORD, the LORD, the compassionate and gracious God, slow to anger, abounding in love and faithfulness, maintaining love to thousands, and forgiving wickedness, rebellion and sin. Yet he does not leave the guilty unpunished; he punishes the children and their children for the sin of the fathers to the third and fourth generation."

Moses bowed to the ground at once and worshiped. (Exodus 33:12–34:8)

17. Moses asked God to show him His glory. What did he mean by glory?

18. Why did Moses ask this?

19. What did God reveal about Himself in response to Moses' request?

20. Part of an intimate relationship is physical contact—a hug when comfort is needed or a hand held in silent support. Just being with another person and seeing the expressions on his or her face can help build intimacy. Why then can't we see God?

21. a. Why do you think God has chosen not to let us see His face?

    b. Does that make it harder for you to know Him? Why or why not?

22. What does it mean to you that God knows you by name? That He invites you to call Him by name?

23. Think back to the "On Your Own" study. Which of the names of God do you most appreciate? Which one do you least identify with right now?

Let's Act (15 minutes)
24. Think back to the names and characteristics of God you have just read about. As you reflect on where you are in life and what you're facing, think of something revealed about God in Scripture that demonstrates what role He might play in your life. Assign Him a creative name related to your current circumstances and explain your thinking to the group.

25. In what ways will the names and characteristics of God that you have just learned impact:

☐ Your worship

☐ Your relationships as a group

☐ Your relationships with others (neighbors, coworkers, family, friends, new believers, disciples, enemies, et cetera).

 GROUP WORSHIP   **(15-30 minutes)**

26. Read Psalm 8 together.

O LORD, our Lord,
>   how majestic is your name in all the earth!

You have set your glory above the heavens.
From the lips of children and infants you have ordained
>   praise
because of your enemies, to silence the foe and the avenger.
When I consider your heavens, the work of your fingers,
the moon and the stars, which you have set in place,
what is man that you are mindful of him,
>   the son of man that you care for him?
You made him a little lower than the heavenly beings
>   and crowned him with glory and honor.
You made him ruler over the works of your hands;
>   you put everything under his feet:
all flocks and herds, and the beasts of the field,

the birds of the air, and the fish of the sea,
   all that swim the paths of the seas.

O LORD, our Lord,
   how majestic is your name in all the earth! (Psalm 8:1-9)

27. If your group is so inclined, sing an appropriate hymn or chorus.

28. Close in prayer. Pick one of God's names revealed in the Bible and focus on it. Praise God that He reveals Himself to you through His names. Ask Him to show you His nature through the name you chose. Pray for any requests that God can meet through the revelation of His character through His different names.

3
LOVING GOD AND LETTING GOD LOVE ME

But God demonstrates his own love for us in this: While we were still sinners, Christ died for us.

—Romans 5:8

 OVERVIEW

What does it mean to love someone? What makes love grow or diminish? And how do we love a God we cannot see or touch?

In this session, we'll examine the nature of love and how we experience and express love with others and with God. By looking at God's expectations of us and our typical responses, we'll gain a deeper understanding of what love for God looks like. Your goal is to be able to accurately describe God's love for us and our love for Him.

So, what's the big deal?

What exactly is love? We profess love for everything from our families to chocolate. Love encompasses a broad range of feelings. So, how does God love us, and how do we respond in love?

 ON YOUR OWN (30-60 minutes)

1. What are some of the things and/or people that you love?

Love plays a foundational role in God's kingdom, as is evidenced in the following passage. In Jesus' day, Jewish rabbis counted 613 individual statutes in the law, and attempted to distinguish between those which were greatest and those which were secondary.

> One of the teachers of the law came and heard them debating. Noticing that Jesus had given them a good answer, he asked him, "Of all the commandments, which is the most important?"
>
> "The most important one," answered Jesus, "is this: 'Hear, O Israel, The Lord our God, the Lord is one. Love the Lord your God with all your heart and with all your soul and with all your mind and with all your strength.' The second is this: 'Love your neighbor as yourself.' There is no commandment greater than these."
>
> "Well said, teacher," the man replied. "You are right in saying that God is one and there is no other but him. To love him with all your heart, with all your understanding and with all your strength, and to love your neighbor as yourself is more important than all burnt offerings and sacrifices." (Mark 12:28-33)

2. What does it look like to love God with . . .

☐ your heart?

☐ your soul?

☐ your mind?

☐ your strength?

3. Why do you think that this commandment is the greatest?

4. How does loving your neighbor as yourself play into your love for God?

5. Why does God value our loving Him more than our making sacrifices for Him?

In Luke 10:25-37, Jesus tells a parable to demonstrate how to love our neighbor as ourselves. The three characters in the parable have special significance to Jesus' audience. Priests were the religious leaders of the day, and Levites were their lay associates. Samaritans were hated and viewed by the Jews as half-breeds, both physically and spiritually (see 2 Kings 17:24-41). Samaritans and Jews were openly hostile to one another, and for them to help each other was practically unheard of.

On one occasion an expert in the law stood up to test Jesus. "Teacher," he asked, "What must I do to inherit eternal life?"

"What is written in the Law?" he replied. "How do you read it?"

He answered: "'Love the Lord your God with all your heart and with all your soul and with all your strength and with all your mind'; and, 'Love your neighbor as yourself.'"

"You have answered correctly," Jesus replied. "Do this and you will live."

But he wanted to justify himself, so he asked Jesus, "And who is my neighbor?"

In reply Jesus said: "A man was going down from Jerusalem to Jericho, when he fell into the hands of robbers. They stripped him of his clothes, beat him and went away, leaving him half dead. A priest happened to be going down the same road, and when he saw the man, he passed by on the other side. So too, a Levite, when he came to the place and saw him, passed by on the other side. But a Samaritan, as he traveled, came where the man was; and when he saw him, he took pity on him. He went to him and bandaged his wounds, pouring on oil and wine. Then he put the man on his own donkey, took him to an inn and took care of him. The next day he took out two silver coins and gave them to the innkeeper. 'Look after him,' he said, 'and when I return, I will reimburse you for any extra expense you may have.'

"Which of these three do you think was a neighbor to the man who fell into the hands of robbers?"

The expert in the law replied, "The one who had mercy on him." Jesus told him, "Go and do likewise." (Luke 10:25-37)

6. Why do you think the expert in the law "wanted to justify himself"?

The road from Jerusalem to Jericho was steep and craggy. Robbers often hid and waited for travelers to come by in order to steal from them. Also, according to Jewish law, contact with a corpse made a person ritually unclean—unable to participate in the temple worship without taking considerable time and effort to become clean again.

7. Why do you think the priest and the Levite passed by?

8. Knowing the danger of hiding bandits and the inconvenience of ritual uncleaness, what do you think you would have done had you encountered the man?

9. What does it mean to "take pity" on someone?

10. The Samaritan went out of his way to care for the beaten man. He not only took him to the inn, but "took care of him." He paid the innkeeper two silver coins (the equivalent of two days' wages) for the man's long-term care, and offered to pay any extra expenses when he returned. What are some opportunities you have to love your neighbor in this way?

11. How are mercy and love related?

GROUP DISCOVERY   (50-90 minutes)

Let's Warm Up (10 minutes)

12. How is love portrayed in the media?

13. Do you think the media is generally accurate or inaccurate? Explain your answer?

Let's Talk (30-50 minutes)

14. Discuss the "On Your Own" questions. What did you learn about loving God? About loving your neighbor?

The Bible is full of information about love (God Himself is love). The word "love" appears forty-three times in the short book of 1 John. Have someone read 1 John 4:7–5:3 before answering the following questions.

15. How does John describe love? What is its source?

16. How has God shown His love for us?

17. John names several things we should do in response. What are they?

18. John says that there is no fear in love. Do you have fears about God's love? If so, what are they?
    □ I'm afraid God will stop loving me.
    □ I'm afraid that if I sin "really big," God will punish me.
    □ I'm afraid God's love means that He'll be more active in my everyday life.
    □ I'm afraid I'm not good enough for God's love.
    □ I'm afraid God's love is just something abstract that doesn't really make any difference in this life.
    □ Other (please explain):

19. Where do you think those fears come from?

20. One way to better understand God's love is to compare it with human love. Take five minutes to brainstorm a list of words that describe God's love and human love.

GOD'S LOVE | HUMAN LOVE

21. How would you summarize the differences between God's love and human love?

22. How will you rely on the love God has for you?
    ☐ I trust God to take care of my problems and concerns.
    ☐ I stop worrying over little things.
    ☐ I pray and expect God to answer.
    ☐ I show others God's love through my words and actions.
    ☐ I'm not quite there yet; give me some time.
    ☐ Other (please explain):

23. What are some ways in which you can express your love for God?

Let's Act (15 minutes)

24. Perhaps the most recognized passage about love in the Bible is found in 1 Corinthians 13. Read verses 1-13 and make a list of the words Paul uses to describe love.

25. How would the practice of this kind of love affect your experience as a group?

26. What are some ways you want to grow in love? How can you help one another in this endeavor?

27. How does God's love for you (and yours for Him) affect these things?

    ☐ Your worship

    ☐ Your relationships as a group

    ☐ Your responsibilities/relationships with others (neighbors, coworkers, family, friends, new believers, disciples, enemies, et cetera).

28. Read 1 Corinthians 13:4-8 again as a group.

Love is patient, love is kind. It does not envy, it does not
boast, it is not proud. It is not rude, it is not self-seeking, it
is not easily angered, it keeps no record of wrongs. Love
does not delight in evil but rejoices with the truth. It always
protects, always trusts, always hopes, always perseveres.
Love never fails. (1 Corinthians 13:4-8)

29. If your group is so inclined, sing an appropriate hymn or chorus.

30. If you feel comfortable, hold hands as you close in prayer. In short
sentences, tell God what you love about Him and ask Him for
help in loving one another. Don't set a time limit, but instead have
someone close as the Spirit leads.

4
GOD'S INVITATION TO INTIMACY

I will walk among you and be your God, and you will be my people.

—Leviticus 26:12

OVERVIEW

God has no favorites, but His relationship is more intimate with some people than with others. God has invited us to get to know Him in a variety of ways. When we take Him up on His invitations, the result is intimacy. The dictionary defines intimacy as "a close acquaintance or friendship, personal, detailed knowledge obtained by study or experience." Intimacy is a natural outgrowth of relationships that are built on trust.

In this session, we will look at some of the ways that God invites us to know Him better. By examining passages in both the Old and New Testaments, we'll get a better understanding of how we can know God. Your goal is to identify ways to know God and examine your own responses to God's invitations to intimacy.

So, what's the big deal?
It's not obvious how we can be intimate with someone we cannot see or touch. What are some of the ways God uses to build intimacy with us, and how can we respond to them?

ON YOUR OWN (30-60 minutes)

1. What words come to mind when you think of intimacy?

2. How would you describe your own experiences of intimacy?

3. Think about intimacy with God. Which statement most accurately describes your feelings about an intimate relationship with God?
   - ☐ It sounds too good to be true, so it probably is.
   - ☐ It's hard to believe that the God of the universe really wants to have that kind of relationship with me.
   - ☐ I'd love to develop that kind of relationship with God, but I'm not sure where to start.
   - ☐ I would describe my relationship with God as intimate and want it to keep growing.
   - ☐ Other (please explain):

God does desire to have an intimate relationship with each one of us, His children. Abram (later called Abraham) is a good example of God's interest in our lives and of His invitation to build intimacy with Him.

> The LORD had said to Abram, "Leave your country, your people and your father's household and go to the land I will show you.
>   "I will make you into a great nation
>   and I will bless you;
>   I will make your name great,
>   and you will be a blessing.
>   I will bless those who bless you,

46

and whoever curses you I will curse;
and all peoples on earth
will be blessed through you."

So Abram left, as the LORD had told him; and Lot went with him. Abram was seventy-five years old when he set out from Haran. He took his wife Sarai, his nephew Lot, all the possessions they had accumulated and the people they had acquired in Haran, and they set out for the land of Canaan, and they arrived there.

Abram traveled through the land as far as the site of the great tree of Moreh at Shechem. At that time the Canaanites were in the land. The LORD appeared to Abram and said, "To your offspring I will give this land." So he built an altar there to the LORD, who had appeared to him. (Genesis 12:1-7)

4. What did God promise Abram?

5. How would you describe the kind of relationship God proposed to have with Abram?

6. How did Abram respond to God?

As believers and Abraham's spiritual descendants, we share in God's promise to be our God. Throughout the Old Testament, God reminds His people of His faithfulness and promises to them. In Leviticus, God reviews how He has upheld His promises.

I will walk among you and be your God, and you will be my people. (Leviticus 26:12)

During the time Israel spent wandering in the desert, God lived among them in different ways. He appeared to them as a cloud during the day and as a pillar of fire at night. This visible manifestation of God guided the people as they traveled, showing them when to stop and when to continue on their journey. Another way in which God was present with them was through the tabernacle. The tabernacle was a special tent designed by God to be His own dwelling. There the people worshiped God and offered sacrifices. The tabernacle could be compared to a modern church.

7. What are some of the ways in which God lives among us today?

8. How do you typically respond to these evidences? Do you barely notice them or count them as invitations from God to know Him better?

It's hard to imagine getting to know someone without eating together. Eating together provides a relaxed atmosphere to build trust and share our lives with others.

God invites us to eat with Him as well. Throughout the Gospels, we see Jesus eating with His disciples and followers. One of His most famous miracles—the feeding of the five thousand—happened at mealtime.

Perhaps the most well-known meal Jesus ate with His disciples is the Lord's Supper. After entering Jerusalem, Jesus and the disciples prepared to celebrate the Passover. Passover is a yearly celebration to remember how God rescued Israel from Egypt (see Exodus 12).

On the first day of the Feast of Unleavened Bread, the disciples came to Jesus and asked, "Where do you want us to make preparations for you to eat the Passover?"

He replied, "Go into the city to a certain man and tell him,

'The Teacher says: My appointed time is near. I am going to celebrate the Passover with my disciples at your house.'" So the disciples did as Jesus had directed them and prepared the Passover.

When evening came, Jesus was reclining at the table with the Twelve. And while they were eating, he said, "I tell you the truth, one of you will betray me."

They were very sad and began to say to him one after the other, "Surely not I, Lord?"

Jesus replied, "The one who has dipped his hand into the bowl with me will betray me. The Son of Man will go just as it is written about him. But woe to that man who betrays the Son of Man! It would be better for him if he had not been born."

Then Judas, the one who would betray him, said, "Surely not I, Rabbi?"

Jesus answered, "Yes, it is you."

While they were eating, Jesus took bread, gave thanks and broke it, and gave it to his disciples, saying, "Take and eat; this is my body."

Then he took the cup, gave thanks and offered it to them, saying, "Drink from it, all of you. This is my blood of the covenant, which is poured out for many for the forgiveness of sins. I tell you, I will not drink of this fruit of the vine from now on until that day when I drink it anew with you in my Father's kingdom."

When they had sung a hymn, they went out to the Mount of Olives. (Matthew 26:17-30)

9. How did Jesus and His disciples celebrate the Passover?

10. What was the deeper meaning behind the Lord's Supper?

11. How can celebrating the Lord's Supper (also called communion) foster intimacy with God?

For Further Study
In Isaiah 1:18, God invites us to reason with Him. Why do you think God wants to reason with us? How is this an invitation to build intimacy with God? What are some other ways God invites us to know Him better?

GROUP DISCOVERY   **(50-90 minutes)**

Let's Warm Up (10 minutes)
12. What are some of the ways we make friends? How do we get to know people better?

Let's Talk (30-50 minutes)
13. Discuss the "On Your Own" questions. What did you learn about God? About intimacy? About yourself?

One of the ways we get to know others is by learning about their likes and dislikes, their strengths and characteristics. God invites us to get to know Him in a similar way through worship.

Worship can be described as "reverence and respect paid to God, adoration or devotion." Part of worship is acknowledging that God is who He says He is and that He has the power to fulfill His promises.

On His way to Galilee, Jesus traveled through Samaria. Jews normally detoured around Samaria because of the hostility between

Samaritans and Jews. As Jesus stopped for a drink, He met a woman who tried to draw Jesus away from His revelation of her life by engaging Him in a discussion about worship.

> He told her, "Go, call your husband and come back."
> "I have no husband," she replied.
> Jesus said to her, "You are right when you say you have no husband. The fact is, you have had five husbands, and the man you now have is not your husband. What you have just said is quite true."
> "Sir," the woman said, "I can see that you are a prophet. Our fathers worshiped on this mountain, but you Jews claim that the place where we must worship is in Jerusalem."
> Jesus declared, "Believe me, woman, a time is coming when you will worship the Father neither on this mountain nor in Jerusalem. You Samaritans worship what you do not know; we worship what we do know, for salvation is from the Jews. Yet a time is coming and has now come when the true worshipers will worship the Father in spirit and truth, for they are the kind of worshipers the Father seeks. God is spirit, and his worshipers must worship in spirit and in truth."
> The woman said, "I know that Messiah" (called Christ) "is coming. When he comes, he will explain everything to us."
> Then Jesus declared, "I who speak to you am he."
> (John 4:16-26)

14. What issue regarding worship was the woman focused on?

15. What kind of worship did Jesus say God desires?

16. What do you think it means to worship God in spirit? In truth?

17. How does worshiping God develop intimacy?

18. Are there times when you feel closer to God in worship than others?

Another way we get to know people and develop intimacy with them is through conversation. Prayer is conversation with God. We often hear prayer described as simply talking to God. As easy as that sounds, the disciples weren't sure how to pray—even after spending so much time with Jesus, who was God on earth! When they asked for a lesson in prayer, Jesus responded with these observations:

> "And when you pray, do not be like the hypocrites, for they love to pray standing in the synagogues and on the street corners to be seen by men. I tell you the truth, they have received their reward in full. But when you pray, go into your room, close the door and pray to your Father, who is unseen. Then your Father, who sees what is done in secret, will reward you. And when you pray, do not keep on babbling like pagans, for they think they will be heard because of their many words. Do not be like them, for your Father knows what you need before you ask him.
> "This, then, is how you should pray:
>
> "'Our Father in heaven,
> hallowed be your name,
> your kingdom come,
> your will be done
> on earth as it is in heaven.
> Give us today our daily bread.

Forgive us our debts,
as we also have forgiven our debtors.
And lead us not into temptation,
but deliver us from the evil one.'" (Matthew 6:5-13)

19. How does Jesus say we should pray?

20. Compare the way Jesus says we should pray with the way the hypocrites pray. Which is more conducive to intimacy and why?

21. Read the Lord's Prayer aloud. Which words or ideas strike you as being "intimate"?

22. Has prayer deepened your relationship with God?

Let's Act (15 minutes)

23. Think about some of the ways God invites us to deeper intimacy with Him. How can this group build intimacy using some of these same ideas?
    - ☐ Eat together before beginning each week's lesson.
    - ☐ Pray aloud together.
    - ☐ Spend time in each other's homes.
    - ☐ Celebrate the Lord's Supper together.
    - ☐ Worship God together.
    - ☐ Other (please explain):

24. What are some ways this group can help you develop deeper intimacy with God?

Let's Worship (15 minutes)

Design your own worship time based on the material in this lesson. Close by praying the Lord's Prayer together.

Let's Listen to God (15 minutes)

Throughout this study guide the question, "What do you think the Holy Spirit is saying to your group about . . . ?" is raised. Perhaps it seems presumptuous to claim to know what the Spirit is saying. Perhaps you are confident that you know, or maybe you are willing to settle for what you think the Spirit *ought* to be saying to your group.

Listening to the Spirit's voice is a skill your group can develop over time. It requires discipline and the willingness to cultivate certain attitudes and take certain risks. As you begin your time of listening to God, read aloud the following commitments. These are not once-for-all-time commitments; each one will require a process of commitment and recommitment by each group member.

▶ We acknowledge our own agendas, plans, philosophies, ideas, and paradigms, and we determine not to let them interfere with our relationship with God or with each other. We may not get this right all the time, but will keep it in mind every week as we meet.

▶ We commit ourselves to being open, honest, vulnerable, available, and transparent. Of course, if we're going to do this for real, we will have to deal with the relationship tensions and conflicts that arise. The result will be the beginning of authentic relationships.

▶ We present ourselves to God in humility, poverty of spirit, brokenness, contrition, and submission. God says He is near to these kinds of persons (Isaiah 57:15, 66:2). The prophet Azariah told the king and people of Judah:

> "The LORD is with you when you are with him. If you seek him, he will be found by you, but if you forsake him, he will forsake you. For a long time Israel was without the true God. . . . But in their distress they turned to the LORD, the God of Israel, and sought him, and he was found by them." (2 Chronicles 15:1-4)

Your agenda for this time of listening to God is to try to hear what God is saying through each group member as you share your thoughts on the following questions. Your challenge is to listen to God while talking to each other. Take a moment for silent prayer, then spend about fifteen minutes on the following:

25. After reading aloud the preceding three commitments, discuss what you sense the Holy Spirit is communicating to your group about the following areas.

    ☐ Your worship and relationship with God

    ☐ Your relationships with each other

    ☐ Your relationships with those outside this group

Take a moment to close this conversation in prayer.

5

TELLING THE STORY

*Hear, O Israel: The L*ORD *our God, the L*ORD *is one.*
                                    —*Deuteronomy 6:4*

![globe icon] **OVERVIEW**

One of the characteristics of intimate relationships is that we dwell on them and tell others about them. Parents think and talk about their children, wives about their husbands, and friends about each other.

A key word in the book of Deuteronomy is "remember." In Deuteronomy 8:2 Moses tells the Israelites to "Remember how the LORD your God led you all the way in the desert these forty years. . . . " Remembering God's faithfulness in the past helps us grow in intimacy with Him.

In this session, we will remember how God has worked in our lives and share our stories of God's faithfulness with each other. Your goal is to recall those times of close fellowship with God and learn how remembering them builds intimacy.

So, what's the big deal?
By observing how God has worked in my life in the past, I can grow in my relationship with Him today.

 ON YOUR OWN   **(30-60 minutes)**

1. What is a memory?

2. Why are memories important?

Some things are easier to remember than others. Each of us learns in a different way and remembers things differently. One way to remember something is to repeat it over and over.

The *Shema* (Hebrew for "hear") is a confession of faith recited by Jews. Pious Jews recite the *Shema* every day, bringing to mind God's faithfulness to them.

> Hear, O Israel: The LORD our God, the LORD is one. Love the LORD your God with all your heart and with all your soul and with all your strength. These commandments that I give you today are to be upon your hearts. Impress them on your children. Talk about them when you sit at home and when you walk along the road, when you lie down and when you get up. Tie them as symbols on your hands and bind them on your foreheads. Write them on the doorframes of your houses and on your gates.
> (Deuteronomy 6:4-9)

3. What other ways of remembering are mentioned in the *Shema?*

4. How do you think reciting the *Shema* affected the Israelites?

The rest of your preparation time will be spent preparing your own "shema"—the story of how God has worked in your life. The idea of putting your story down on paper and sharing it with a group can be difficult. The following guidelines are designed to help you think through how God has worked in your life and how best to share your story with the group.

5. Think through the following times in your life. How was God involved in your life? (Possibilities include significant memories, major decisions, life-changing events, or times of growth.)

☐ Childhood

☐ Adolescence

☐ Early adulthood

☐ Adulthood

6. As you look back over what you wrote, how has God used adversity in your life? (This could be hard times, trauma, pain, defeat, failure, et cetera.)

7. How has God used times of blessing? (This could be success, happy times, rewards, et cetera.)

8. What have you learned about God's character?

9. How does God get your attention?

10. How have you responded to those times?

11. What is one truth about God that you hold most closely?

12. As you think about sharing the story of God's work in your life, what is one thing that you'd like the members of your group to know about God?

13. Between now and the time when your group meets, pray for God's guidance and insight into what you share with the rest of the group.

GROUP DISCOVERY (50-90 minutes)

Let's Warm Up (10 minutes)

14. What is one of your favorite memories from childhood? Why?

Let's Talk (30-50 minutes)

This session will be different from previous ones. The goal is to learn more about one another and to hear how God has worked in each other's lives. It can sometimes be intimidating to share with a group. Allow sufficient time for each person to share. If necessary, you may decide to take two group meetings for these stories. Also, you may want to review the group member commitments on pages 54-55.

Let's Act (15 minutes)

15. How were you encouraged by preparing your own story?

16. What new insights into God's desire to be intimate with each one of us did you have by hearing other people's stories? How will you put that insight into action this week?

17. How did preparing and sharing your story build intimacy with each other? With God? What will your group do in the future to build on the intimacy you've begun?

18. Have someone read Psalm 139:1-16 to the group.

19. If your group is so inclined, sing an appropriate hymn or chorus.

20. Close in prayer. Divide into pairs or groups of three. Praise God for the way He has worked in your lives and for His desire to be in relationship with each individual. Share any requests and commit to pray for one another throughout the upcoming week.

Let's Listen to God (15 minutes)

21. After reading aloud the three commitments on pages 54-55, discuss what you sense the Holy Spirit is communicating to your group about the following areas?

    ☐ Your worship and relationship with God

    ☐ Your relationships with each other

    ☐ Your relationships with those outside this group

Take a moment to close this conversation in prayer.

6
INTIMACY ON THE RUN

Be still, and know that I am God.

—Psalm 46:10

Life today is busy. That's all too obvious as we race from one thing to another, frantically bemoaning the fact that we just don't have enough time. We do many things at once—talk on the phone as we drive down the street, watch television while we eat, and help with homework while we cook dinner.

How can we develop intimacy in the midst of all that clamors for our time and attention?

Intimacy is a choice. In this session we will examine the nature of our busyness and those things that demand our time. Your goal is to identify unnecessary priorities and to learn ways to choose intimacy despite the busyness you face.

So, what's the big deal?
There are a million things requiring my time and attention. I want to take the time to develop an intimate relationship with God, but how do I adjust my overloaded lifestyle to make that possible?

ON YOUR OWN   **(30-60 minutes)**

1. What do you think of when you hear the word "busy"?

63

2. Why do you think we are so busy?
   ☐ We measure our worth by how much we have to do.
   ☐ We're afraid that if we're not busy, we're not shouldering our
      fair share of responsibility.
   ☐ We fear boredom.
   ☐ We're afraid to say no to others' expectations of us.
   ☐ It makes us feel good to be needed.
   ☐ That's just how life works these days. There's no way around it.
   ☐ Other (please explain):

The story of Mary and Martha illustrates our attitudes about busyness.
Read the story below, underlining anything that stands out to you.

> As Jesus and his disciples were on their way, he came to a village
> where a woman named Martha opened her home to him. She had
> a sister called Mary, who sat at the Lord's feet listening to what he
> said. But Martha was distracted by all the preparations that had to
> be made. She came to him and asked, "Lord, don't you care that
> my sister has left me to do the work by myself? Tell her to help
> me!"
> "Martha, Martha," the Lord answered, "you are worried and
> upset about many things, but only one thing is needed. Mary has
> chosen what is better, and it will not be taken away from her."
> (Luke 10:38-42)

3. What upset Martha?

4. How did Jesus respond?

5. Do you relate more to Martha or Mary? Why?

6. Luke says Martha was "distracted." What are some of the things that distract you from God?

7. Jesus said Martha was "worried and upset about many things." Often it's the little things that can draw us away from intimacy with God. In your list above, underline the important matters and circle the little things.

8. What would it cost you to make time to sit at Jesus' feet regularly? What would you have to give up or risk? (Or, if you are already taking time regularly, what does that cost you?)

9. Mary probably had worries too, yet she chose to sit at Jesus' feet when she had the opportunity. What would you recommend to a person who has trouble making that choice consistently?

For Further Study

In the midst of hectic schedules and too much to do, it sometimes helps to set aside time to sit at Jesus' feet as Mary did. This time with God (often called a quiet time) can be spent anywhere and at any time of the day. If you're not currently spending some time alone with God each day, it may be helpful to commit just five minutes of your day to God. It helps to consistently make those the same five minutes each day—for example, either when you first wake up or before you go to sleep.

If you're already spending time with God on a daily basis, it can be a good idea to begin setting aside larger chunks of time every once in a while. A few hours on a Saturday morning or Sunday afternoon can be spent quietly conversing with God and deepening your relationship with Him.

 GROUP DISCOVERY (50-90 minutes)

Let's Warm Up (10 minutes)

10. When you go on vacation, do you take things to do, or are you content to rest and relax?

Let's Talk (30-50 minutes)

11. Discuss the "On Your Own" questions. What did you learn about intimacy? About God? About yourself?

12. How prone are you to worry?
    ☐ I worry about everything.
    ☐ I worry about big things.
    ☐ I worry about not getting everything done that I'm supposed to.
    ☐ I worry about the people in my life.
    ☐ I don't worry very much.
    ☐ Other:

In the Sermon on the Mount, Jesus addressed the futility of worry. Have someone read the following passage out loud.

> "Therefore I tell you, do not worry about your life, what you will eat or drink; or about your body, what you will wear. Is not life more important than food, and the body more important than clothes? Look at the birds of the air; they do not sow or reap or store away in barns, and yet your heavenly Father feeds them. Are you not much more valuable than they? Who of you by worrying can add a single hour to his life?
>
> "And why do you worry about clothes? See how the lilies of the field grow. They do not labor or spin. Yet I tell you that not even Solomon in all his splendor was dressed like one of these. If that is how God clothes the grass of the field, which is here today and tomorrow is thrown into the fire, will he not much more clothe you, O you of little faith? So do not worry, saying, 'What shall we eat?' or 'What shall we drink?' or 'What shall we wear?' For the pagans run after all these things, and your heavenly Father knows that you need them. But seek first his kingdom and his righteousness, and all these things will be given to you as well. Therefore do not worry about tomorrow, for tomorrow will worry about itself. Each day has enough trouble of its own."
> (Matthew 6:25-34)

13. What kinds of things does Jesus say we shouldn't worry about?

14. Why shouldn't we worry?

15. Why does Jesus tell us that God knows we need the things we worry about?

16. What does Jesus say is the key to avoiding worry?

17. What does it mean to seek God's kingdom first?

18. Think back to the list you made of those things that get in the way of your relationship with God. What would it mean, in practical terms, for you to put God first in that list? How would your life be different?

    ☐ Costs

    ☐ Benefits

19. Many people spend lots of time reading the Bible, praying, or attending church services and small groups without experiencing intimacy with God. Why do you think that is?

20. Are there times when you feel more intimate with God than others? Describe what makes the difference.

21. What most often gets in the way of your experiencing intimacy with God?

22. What is most helpful to experiencing intimacy with God?

23. Is there a relationship between the quantity of time you spend with God and the quality of your intimacy with Him? What makes you say that?

Let's Act (15 minutes)
24. What will you do this week to take the next step in deepening your intimacy with God as a result of this discussion?

25. How can this group help you make intimacy with God a priority?

26. What will you need from this group in order to deal with the worries that get in the way of your relationship with God?

27. Psalm 42:1-2 provides a good example of the desire to experience intimacy with God. Read it together, pausing to reflect on each verse.

> As the deer pants for streams of water,
>   so my soul pants for you, O God.
> My soul thirsts for God, for the living God.
>   When can I go and meet with God? (Psalm 42:1-2)

28. Divide into pairs or groups of three and close in prayer. Thank God that He knows all your worries and needs and will provide. Pray for help in seeking His kingdom first and thirsting to know Him in a deeper and more intimate way.

Let's Listen to God (15 minutes)
Read aloud the three commitments on pages 54-55.

29. After reading aloud the three commitments on pages 54-55, discuss what you sense the Holy Spirit is communicating to your group about the following areas?

☐ Your worship and relationship with God

☐ Your relationships with each other

☐ Your relationships with those outside this group

Take a moment to close this conversation in prayer.

7
OVERCOMING BARRIERS TO INTIMACY

Open your ears, God, to my prayer;
> *don't pretend you don't hear me knocking.*
Come close and whisper your answer.
> *I really need you.*
>> —*Psalm 55:1-2, from* The Message

OVERVIEW

Other things besides busyness can get in the way of developing an intimate relationship. Intimacy is sometimes defined as "emotional closeness." If we're absent emotionally when we meet with God, chances are that intimacy won't develop. Unless we can be completely honest with God (and ourselves) about our emotions, we won't develop the kind of intimate relationship God has invited us to experience with Him.

In this session, we will look at the Psalms as examples of the kind of honest expression of emotions necessary to develop an intimate relationship with God. We will also examine the Scriptures to find other barriers to intimacy. Your goal is to identify ways to communicate your emotions with God and to overcome barriers that hinder your closeness with God.

So, what's the big deal?
Some of us aren't good at being emotionally available to anyone. And even the most emotionally mature of us may wonder how to respond from the heart to an invisible, all-powerful being. Does involving our emotions in intimacy with God mean sloppy sentimentality, hyped feelings, or what?

71

ON YOUR OWN (30-60 minutes)

1. Make a list of the emotions you're aware of feeling during a typical week.

2. Are you more of a thinking person or a feeling person? (In general, when you approach a situation, do you think it through, or act on the way you feel about it?)

3. On a scale of 1 to 10, how comfortable are you with expressing your feelings (1=not comfortable at all; 10=very comfortable)?

1	2	3	4	5	6	7	8	9	10
not comfortable								very comfortable	

4. What do you think about being totally honest with God?
   - ☐ I'm very honest with God even though He already knows what I'm thinking and feeling. Sometimes it helps just to get it out in the open.
   - ☐ There are some things I don't tell God. I guess He already knows, but I don't want to say them to Him.
   - ☐ I don't know that I could be totally honest with God. I wouldn't want to hurt His feelings or make Him angry.
   - ☐ What's the point? He knows anyway.
   - ☐ How can I be totally honest with God when I'm not even sure how to be honest with myself?
   - ☐ Other (please explain):

The Psalms are great examples of honesty with God. Anger, joy, happiness, despair, helplessness, outrage—just about every emotion can be found.

The Psalms are also examples of deep intimacy with God. No matter what the psalmists were going through, they expressed their feelings to God. The key to such honesty may have been knowing that God could handle any emotion expressed and wouldn't be offended by it.

Read the following psalms from THE MESSAGE, noting the emotions contained in each one.

> I'm thanking you, GOD, from a full heart,
> I'm writing the book on your wonders.
> I'm whistling, laughing, and jumping for joy;
> I'm singing your song, High God. (Psalm 9:1-2, MSG)

4. What emotions is the psalmist feeling?

5. How does praising God with our happiness develop intimacy?

6. What emotions is the psalmist expressing in the following passage?

> Why are you down in the dumps, dear soul?
> Why are you crying the blues?
> Fix my eyes on God—
> soon I'll be praising again.
> He puts a smile on my face.
> He's my God.
>
> When my soul is in the dumps, I rehearse
> everything I know of you,
> From Jordan depths to Hermon heights,
> including Mount Mizar.

Chaos calls to chaos,
    to the tune of whitewater rapids.
Your breaking surf, your thundering breakers
    crash and crush me.
Then God promises to love me all day,
    sing songs all through the night!
    My life is God's prayer.

Sometimes I ask God, my rock-solid God,
    "Why did you let me down?
Why am I walking around in tears,
    harassed by enemies?"
They're out for the kill, these
    tormentors with their obscenities,
Taunting day after day,
    "Where is this God of yours?"

Why are you down in the dumps, dear soul?
    Why are you crying the blues?
Fix my eyes on God—
    soon I'll be praising again.
He puts a smile on my face.
    He's my God. (Psalm 42:5-11, MSG)

7. How does sharing his emotions with God help the psalmist get out of the "dumps"?

8. Has God ever changed your emotions as you've shared your feelings with Him? Describe that experience.

9. What emotions are expressed in the following passage?

> Generous in love—God, give grace!
>> Huge in mercy—wipe out my bad record.
> Scrub away my guilt,
>> soak out my sins in your laundry.
> I know how bad I've been;
>> my sins are staring me down.
>
> You're the One I've violated, and you've seen
>> it all, seen the full extent of my evil.
> You have all the facts before you;
>> whatever you decide about me is fair.
> I've been out of step with you for a long time,
>> in the wrong since before I was born.
> (Psalm 51:1-5, MSG)

10. When you tell God about the sin in your life, do you feel close to God? Why, or why not?

> Open your ears, God, to my prayer;
>> don't pretend you don't hear me knocking.
> Come close and whisper your answer.
>> I really need you.
> I shudder at the mean voice,
>> quail before the evil eye,
> As they pile on the guilt,
>> stockpile angry slander.
>
> My insides are turned inside out;
>> specters of death have me down.
> I shake with fear,
>> I shudder from head to foot.
> "Who will give me wings," I ask—
>> "wings like a dove?"

Get me out of here on dove wings;
    I want some peace and quiet.
I want a walk in the country,
    I want a cabin in the woods.
I'm desperate for a change
    from rage and stormy weather. (Psalm 55:1-8, MSG)

11. Have you ever felt like this psalmist?

12. How do you think the psalmist felt telling God he felt God was ignoring him?

13. What are some ways you express your emotions to God?
- ☐ Singing
- ☐ Talking
- ☐ Yelling
- ☐ Journaling
- ☐ Shouting
- ☐ Whispering
- ☐ Other (please explain):

14. How do you think expressing your feelings to God would develop intimacy with Him?

For Further Study

Start reading a psalm a day. Ask yourself, "What emotions does the psalmist express? When have I felt like that?"

 GROUP DISCOVERY (50-90 minutes)

Let's Warm Up (10 minutes)

15. Do you normally experience or express strong emotions of any kind? Can you discern why or why not?

Let's Talk (30-50 minutes)

16. Discuss the "On Your Own" questions. What did you learn about emotions? About God? About yourself?

17. Think about your relationships with people. What are some of the things that hinder your intimacy with them?

18. Do you think those same things get in the way of intimacy with God? Why, or why not?

The Bible records a number of reasons that we can fail to experience intimacy with God. Sometimes our sinfulness blocks intimacy. At other times, God's silence helps us grow in faith.

Job experienced God's silence. A godly man, Job trusted God completely. Satan saw his trust in God and challenged God to allow him to take away Job's family and possessions. Satan claimed that without his wealth and security, Job would deny God. God agreed to the test, and Job lost his wealth, his children, and his health. His example teaches us how we can respond when we feel God has deserted us. Have someone read each of the passages below aloud.

Then Job replied:

"Even today my complaint is bitter;
    his hand is heavy in spite of my groaning.
If only I knew where to find him [God];
    if only I could go to his dwelling!
I would state my case before him
    and fill my mouth with arguments.
I would find out what he would answer me,
    and consider what he would say.
Would he oppose me with great power?
    No, he would not press charges against me.
There an upright man could present his case before him,
    and I would be delivered forever from my judge.

"But if I go to the east, he is not there;
    if I go to the west, I do not find him.
When he is at work in the north, I do not see him;
    when he turns to the south, I catch no glimpse of him.
But he knows the way that I take;
    when he has tested me, I will come forth as gold.
My feet have closely followed his steps;
    I have kept to his way without turning aside.
I have not departed from the commands of his lips;
    I have treasured the words of his mouth more than my
    daily bread." (Job 23:1-12)

19. How did Job feel?

20. What emotions did he express to God?

21. What did Job want from God?

And Job continued his discourse:

"As surely as God lives, who has denied me justice,
    the Almighty, who has made me taste bitterness of soul,
as long as I have life within me,
    the breath of God in my nostrils,
my lips will not speak wickedness,
    and my tongue will utter no deceit.
I will never admit you are in the right;
    till I die, I will not deny my integrity.
I will maintain my righteousness and never let go of it;
    my conscience will not reproach me as long as I live.

"May my enemies be like the wicked,
    my adversaries like the unjust!
For what hope has the godless when he is cut off,
    when God takes away his life?
Does God listen to his cry
    when distress comes upon him?
Will he find delight in the Almighty?
    Will he call upon God at all times?

"I will teach you about the power of God;
    the ways of the Almighty I will not conceal." (Job 27:1-11)

22. When God didn't answer, how did Job respond?

23. Have you ever felt cut off from God? Describe that experience.

24. How did you respond to God's apparent absence?

25. What do you learn about feeling deserted by God from Job?

26. In Job's case, it wasn't sin that caused God's silence. Has sin ever kept you from hearing God's voice? If so, is that something you're willing to share with the group?

Let's Act (15 minutes)
27. Determine at least one way this group can help you identify and express your emotions.

28. What are some ways you can be accountable to one another to examine barriers to intimacy in each of our lives?

29. Design your own time of worship based on the material in this session.

Let's Listen to God (15 minutes)
Read aloud the commitments on pages 54-55.

30. After reading aloud the three commitments on pages 54-55, discuss what you sense the Holy Spirit is communicating to your group about the following areas?

☐ Your worship and relationship with God

☐ Your relationships with each other

☐ Your relationships with those outside this group

Take a moment to close this conversation in prayer.

8.

LET'S PERSONALIZE INTIMACY WITH GOD

OVERVIEW

In this session and the next, you will review and apply the lessons you have learned in sessions 2–7. In this session you will focus on personal lessons and applications, while session 9 will focus on group applications. As you prepare for your group meeting, remember to pray frequently. Some inventory work will help you select the one key truth from sessions 2–7 that is most urgent for you personally. Then your group will help you think through appropriate action steps and life changes you can pursue. Your goal will be to settle on one key truth and the action you can take to build it into your life.

So what's the big deal?

It's better to be obedient in just one area about which God is convicting you than to fill up a workbook full of good intentions about several truths, none of which you obey or profit from.

ON YOUR OWN   (30-60 minutes)

1. What changes are you beginning to see in your relationship with God as a result of this study?

☐ Any mistakes you are avoiding?

☐ Any attitudes you are changing?

☐ Any areas of new freedom in Christ?

☐ Any changes in the way you view God?

☐ Any new ways you feel or things you do when you spend time with God?

2. Review what you have studied and discussed in sessions 2 through 7. Try to state one or two truths that stand out to you as most important in each session. For example, for session 7 you might write, "Difficulty expressing emotions can hinder intimacy with God."

☐ Session 2

☐ Session 3

☐ Session 4

☐ Session 5

☐ Session 6

☐ Session 7

3. You may have repeated yourself in question 2, circling around the same one or two truths that jump out at you from every session. If so, it may be that the Holy Spirit has put His finger on an area of focus. Take a moment to pray about your list of truths. Put a star beside the one that you think is most important for you to address in the near future. Or, combine several of the truths into one, and state it below. (Don't get sidetracked trying to summarize all of your truths into one overarching thesis. The point is to pick one limited idea that you can reasonably grasp and focus on.)

4. How has this truth affected your thinking and behavior so far?

5. How do you think the Holy Spirit would like this truth to affect your life—your thoughts, feelings, and actions?

Be prepared to share your key truth and its effects with your group. They will help you formulate a plan for integrating that truth into your life and acting on it. They will also help keep you accountable to the degree that you allow them to do so. You're not in this alone!

 GROUP DISCOVERY (50-90 minutes)

Let's Warm Up (10 minutes)

6. What is one thing you have gained from this group during the past seven sessions? What is one thing for which you are grateful?

Let's Talk (45-80 minutes)

Plan your time so that you have at least five minutes for each person to share his or her truth and receive help in formulating a plan of action. Ten minutes each would be even better, but that might require going overtime. Be sure that no one is shortchanged of this opportunity for help.

7. Read to your group your key truth, how it has affected you so far, and how you think the Spirit would like it to affect you. Then, with help from the group, come up with a plan for integrating your key truth into your life. Ask yourselves the following questions as you help each other plan your strategies:

- ☐ Is the key truth clear?
- ☐ What results or outcomes would you like to see from this plan of action?
- ☐ Are the action steps specific and realistic?
- ☐ Not all action steps in the spiritual realm are quantifiable. For example, praying for thirty minutes a day is quantifiable, but genuinely opening your heart to God in prayer is not. How will you know if the changes you are pursuing are really happening?

Here is an example of a plan that is practical, specific, measurable, and clear:

I think my difficulty being intimate with God has to do with priorities and feelings. I rush around so much, it's hard for me to be still. And when I make time to be physically still to spend time with God, I can't get my head to be still. The squirrels inside keep running. When I try to coax them to calm down, I start feeling things I don't like feeling: frustration, anxiety, disappointment. Life is not exactly going the way I would have planned it, and those times of almost-stillness remind me how much I'm blaming God and blaming myself. That's not fun; no wonder I'd rather be busy.

The verse at the top of session 6 leaped out at me: "Be still, and know that I am God." I've decided I'm going to take ten minutes at the end of each day to think about what that verse says. I'm going to think about it over and over, and when thoughts and feelings come up that disturb my stillness, I'm going to write them down and then go back to the verse. I'd like someone in this group to check with me every couple of days to see how it's going.

Write your plan on the top of the next page.

8. List anything you have committed to do for someone else in your group:

9. Use this space to list the other group members' key truths (you will need these to do your personal preparation for session 9):

GROUP WORSHIP   (15-30 minutes)

   10. Design and implement your own time of worship. Be sure to include prayer about your key truth and your plans for applying it.

9.

LET'S GROW TOGETHER IN INTIMACY WITH GOD

OVERVIEW

The work you do this session will be similar to session 8 in that you will review and apply the lessons you have learned in sessions 2–7. In this session your goal is to come up with an application for your whole group, whereas last time the focus was on personal application.

Planning group applications requires hard work. You will be thinking in areas that may be different from anything you have tried before. Six areas have been selected to help you evaluate your group's progress.

So what's the big deal?

If you persevere, you will achieve powerful results. You will be growing not just as individuals but also as a community of believers.

ON YOUR OWN   (30-60 minutes)

Throughout the course of these studies, you have had experiences that contributed to your sense of community. Take a few minutes to assess the progress and contributions your group has made in spiritual sensitivity, worship dynamics, relational intimacy, functional interdependence, mission focus, and sphere of influence. This assessment procedure will help you evaluate your group's progress and help you plan for your future relationships.

1. **Ability to listen to the Holy Spirit.** In a group with high sensitivity to the Spirit, you will observe unity and peace created by the Spirit, or you will observe people allowing the Spirit to disrupt their complacency and challenge their assumptions. On a scale of 1 (low) to 5 (high), how would you rate your group's sensitivity, receptivity, and responsiveness to the Holy Spirit's leadership?

1 low	2	3	4	5 high

2. **Worship dynamics.** God is the central focus in worship. Recall your worship times in the preceding sessions. In a group with "rich" worship dynamics you can expect to find a sense of God's majestic presence with you, variety, and everyone participating and contributing. On a scale of 1 (poor) to 5 (rich), how would you assess the overall quality of your group's worship experience?

1 poor	2	3	4	5 rich

3. **Relational intimacy.** The Bible is full of relational terms such as love, forgiveness, acceptance, reconciliation, and bearing one another's burdens. As you experience these conditions, your group will grow in relational intimacy. Evidences of "deep" intimacy are high levels of trust, vulnerability, transparency, honesty, and mutual commitment. On a scale of 1 (shallow) to 5 (deep), how would you assess your group's level of intimacy?

1 shallow	2	3	4	5 deep

4. **Functional interdependence.** The church is the body of Christ, a living organism with many members. Your small group functions like a system in that body, working interdependently with other systems and their members. Not only that, each member of your group is gifted to perform specific tasks that contribute to the overall internal functions of your group. On a scale of 1 (harsh, grating) to 5 (sweet, synchronized), how well are the members of

your community working together toward a common task, and how harmoniously is your community working alongside others?

1	2	3	4	5
harsh, grating				sweet, synchronized

5. **Mission focus.** Christian communities can easily become self-absorbed. This happens when they turn a deaf ear or a blind eye to what's on God's heart and, instead, focus their attention on themselves. The result is a diminished heart for the world that God loves and gave His Son to die for. God uses groups to reach into every nook and cranny of the world. On a scale of 1 (self-absorbed) to 5 (other-focused), how motivated is your group to looking beyond itself and fulfilling God's mission to reach the world?

1	2	3	4	5
self-absorbed				other-focused

6. **Sphere of influence.** God's mission is global in scope, including all kinds of people—rich and poor, men and women, young and old, Black, White, Hispanic, Asian, et cetera. Although we are to be open to new ministry opportunities, God often calls a community to minister within its specific sphere of influence. This sphere sets limits that sharpen your focus. On a scale of 1 (confused, non-existent) to 5 (sharply focused), how clear is it to your community who God has called you to minister to?

1	2	3	4	5
confused				focused

7. Review all the truths and life applications that you and your fellow group members identified last time. What is the one truth from these studies that you feel is most relevant for your whole group collectively? (This may be different from what is most significant to you personally.)

GROUP DISCOVERY (50-90 minutes)

Let's Warm Up (10 minutes)

8. In what one way has this group helped you grow more intimate with God?

Let's Talk (30-45 minutes)

9. Share progress on personal applications from the last session. Are you helping each other follow through on your commitments? How so? Thank God for the progress He has already made among you.

10. Remember, community building is a process. Some members of your group may desire greater intimacy, and some may feel threatened by the intimacy already achieved. God is still at work in your group in the six areas you assessed on pages 90-91. He is molding you into a vehicle fit for Him to use however He wills. Review the six areas of assessment and compare answers as a group. Pay special attention to major differences in your evaluations. How do you account for these differences?

11. Discuss what each of you thinks is the one significant truth most relevant to your group (identified in question 7). Try to come to a group consensus of the one truth and its implications for your group. To reach that consensus, here are some helpful hints:
   ☐ Begin with prayer, asking God to clarify your thinking.
   ☐ List the truth from each individual on a chart or white board.
   ☐ Look for duplications and related themes. Consolidate and combine where possible.

☐ Build consensus on one truth. Sometimes related thoughts can be combined to better reflect the overall truth but beware of stringing ideas together into a broad, complicated conglomeration.

☐ Don't worry about a perfect statement. Blend the ideas of each person in the group to arrive at the consensus position. (Designate someone in the group who has an aptitude with words to edit for clarity and length. Take the statement home to polish it up, if necessary.)

12. Write your group truth here.

13. Next you will plan how to integrate this truth into your group life, much as you did for each individual group member last time. Your first step will be prayer. Take five minutes to ask God to lead you in this process. You might ask, "Lord, how would you like our group to put this truth into practice?" or "God, what would you like our community to become?" Listen quietly. As you have thoughts or impressions, either make mental notes or jot them down.

14. Write three headings on newsprint or a white board: God, One Another, Others. Under the first heading, list ways in which this truth should affect your group's relationship with God. Under the second heading, list ways in which this truth should affect your relationships with each other, and so on.

God	One Another	Others

15. Now brainstorm a fourth list: things you can do to put this truth into practice in your group. Call out ideas without evaluating or criticizing any of them.

16. After five or ten minutes, stop and sort the ideas into short-range steps and long-range steps. Edit them so that each one is a realistic, doable action that lends itself to accountability. Who will do what, by when, where, and for/with whom? Weed out any impractical ideas. Try to come up with at least one short-range and one long-range step that meet these standards.
    ☐ What is it?
    ☐ Who will do what?
    ☐ By when?
    ☐ Where?
    ☐ For/with whom?

    a. Short-range steps

    b. Long-range steps

Because learning to implement this truth as a community is so important, you should commit yourselves to take as many sessions as needed to work out your group application. Place a higher priority on implementing your plan rather than moving on to another study.

17. Design and implement your own time of worship. Be sure to include prayer about your key truth and your plans for applying it. Also, thank God for what you have received from this study. Celebrate your time together, both your past and your future.

If you set out to identify the core elements of the Christian life, what would your list include?

After ten years of Bible study involving thousands of believers from countries all around the world, The Navigators' SCRIPTURAL ROOTS OF LIFE team saw a few basic themes emerge over and over again:

WORSHIP
Worship: Honoring God in All of Life
(ISBN: 1-57683-007-1; 9 sessions; 96 pages)

COMMUNITY
Relationships: Resolving Conflict and Building Community
(ISBN: 1-57683-023-3; 9 sessions; 96 pages)

INTIMACY WITH GOD
Intimacy: Pursuing Intimacy with God
(ISBN: 1-57683-010-1; 9 sessions; 96 pages)

BECOMING LIKE CHRIST
Christlikeness: Committing Ourselves to be Changed by God
(ISBN: 1-57683-006-3; 9 sessions; 96 pages)

THE TRINITY
Restoration: Discovering How God Meets Our Deepest Needs
(ISBN: 1-57683-009-8; 9 sessions; 96 pages)

THE UNSEEN WORLD
Warfare: Discovering the Reality of the Unseen World
(ISBN: 1-57683-026-8; 9 sessions; 96 pages)

SHARING THE FAITH
Outreach: Sharing the Real Gospel with the World
(ISBN: 1-57683-012-8; 9 sessions; 96 pages)

WORK
Work: Serving God on the Job
(ISBN: 1-57683-024-1; 9 sessions; 96 pages)

Designed to foster close-knit community within your group, the FOUNDATIONS FOR CHRISTIAN LIVING series is a great way to grow strong in faith, life, and love for God. Available at your local Christian bookstore. Or call 1-800-366-7788 to order.

NAVPRESS
BRINGING TRUTH TO LIFE